Chapter 1

Beth lay in bed, naked, drowning in a sea of white damp, crumpled sheets, cheap vodka and pills. She lay flat on her stomach, all life drained out of her. Her long blonde hair was matted to her face, her tattooed arm was limp. She felt herself sinking down into a black hole, she wanted to die. What use was living anymore? She had forgotten sunrises and rainbows and love. She felt unloved and ugly, there was nothing but emptiness now. Death was finally at her door. She drank one more glass of vodka to wash down the Oxycontins in her hand. She was Marilyn, tragic and beautiful.

"Please let me die." she whispered. But no one was there.

It was time to go. She felt herself floating…..She could hear an angels voice in her ear, whispering to her. She could feel the roar of a mighty wind blowing her dingy to a distant shore…..

It was yet another night in a loud, smoky bar in South Florida. We band wives were relegated to a booth in the corner while our mates played on stage. I was married to Phil "The Preacher,"drummer, Stephanie was married to Ian "The Stoner," bass player and Beth was dating Jon "The Lover," guitar player. The band was rocking tonight.

Two skanky girls in skintight spandex dresses began dancing together in front of the band. The guys were definitely checking out the leg and breast action in front of them, their lesbo fantasies abounding. Smiles stretched across their faces as they tried to look cool.

I looked at Stephanie and raised my eyebrows. “See that?”

“Yup”. She sipped her drink, staring at the obscene scene unfolding before us.

“He would never let me out of the house in that getup. But he sure digs it on her. Look at the smiles on their faces…” I said. They all that goopy look on their faces.

“Men, they are strange.” she mused.

“Hypocrites.” I added.

“Chauvinists. The double standard still exists.”…..she ventured to say.

I agreed. The two voluptuous chicks continued their bumping and grinding until it was time for the band to take a set break. The guys came and joined us at our table. It was a sanctuary from the crowd. My husband was definitely buzzed out of his mind from the Captain Morgan and Coke. He reached over into my pocketbook, the large bag that housed the flask with the illicite hooch in it.

“Quick, give me another shot.” Phil said.

“Alright, is anybody coming?” I looked around nervously. You didn’t want to get caught with your own shit in a bar. It was a definite no-no. Not to mention illegal.

“No….Hurry up.”

I poured a decent shot into his glass. I didn’t like him getting so wasted but it mellowed him out, like Zanex for the soul. Phil was a good husband, loyal, loving, talented and a musician to his very core. I didn’t mind sitting around for hours while he played. It got boring sometimes hearing the same songs over and over again, but so what? It was better than staying home. Sort of…..Although sometimes I wouldn’t mind staying home and cleaning out my closet or organizing the kitchen. But I usually came to the gigs. I was his roady after all. Somehow I got suckered into carrying his gear due to his double hernia….

The guys talked shop. It was a never-ending conversation about tone, loudness and who fucked up which song. Seems like tonight Jon was the bad guy, speeding up all the songs. I tried to get Phil’s attention but he was engrossed in band talk, which left me feeling somewhat neglected. Maybe I should don a sexy outfit and dance the maiden dance in front of the band, maybe that would get his attention. That’s a laugh!

The guys went back to play the last set. Stephanie and I were deep in conversation about our love lives. Stephanie was a five foot five inch fiery redhead with a blunt haircut.

She weighed about two hundred pounds, had a beautiful face and hazel eyes.

“I feel like something’s missing in my life.” murmured Stephanie.

“What do you mean?” I asked.

“Well, it’s kind of embarrassing….” She sighed.

“If you’d rather not say anything…”

“What I mean is…Since…Since, the weight….” She hesitated….“Since the weight, Ian hasn’t been as turned on by me anymore.”

“Really?” I choked on my soda.

“Yeah, I’ve been on a diet but nothing helps.”

“Have you tried some sexy lingerie? A porno movie? Or scented candles?”

“I have tried everything. Sex with us is just a chore for him. He says only skinny girls turn him on. He says it’s a visual thing. Some shit like that…”

“Right. It’s all in their heads. Men are such pricks. I don’t know what porn they are looking at, but they all must watch the same thing. Some ninety-pound chick doing another ninety-pound chick or some shit like that. It's totally manufactured garbage. Those women are not real. They don't have real needs. They never ask for or need anything."

"Tell me about it. They don't have to do the work. They never get PMS…They just get the reward."

"Exactly. I have the same issues with Phil. He keeps pointing out to me how fat I am. I am really getting pretty tired of it. I told him to find a new hundred pound girlfriend. There's a ton of anorexic supermodels on crack out there. But I'll bet they would be too worried about breaking a fingernail while moving his shit."

It was true. I had also gained some weight. I was five foot eight inches, weighed about one seventy-five and counting and was far from the one hundred and twenty pound beauty he had discovered a decade ago. I called it getting older. He called it getting fatter. Either way, it was no good for our ailing love life.

My self-esteem was at an all time low; it wasn't easy changing clothes in the fitting rooms anymore or going to the beach. I was conscious of the weight. I tried to diet but it was hard. All these late night gigs. We'd get hungry and stop at Wendy's for a late night snack of fries and chicken wraps and wash it all down with tons of Coke. My diet sucked. Living the life of a working musician meant lots of meals on the go, late nights, smoke filled bars and generally unhealthy stuff. It wasn't like I could survive on salads and juices, or have the money to have those low cal gourmet meals delivered like celebrities did.

"I am getting pretty tired of it." Stephanie said

"I hear you girlfriend…I guess you can always try the E word…Exercise…."

"I'm doing four hours a day." Her voice rose to a fever pitch.

"Really? Are you kidding me?" I gasped.

"No. I bought this tape, it's really good. I can feel my legs getting all stretched out and my arms hurt. It kills me…."

"That's good…We've been golfing. I've been walking five miles a day! Now that's some exercise, walking eighteen holes and chasing a stupid ball. I am sure that golf was invented by men, because women could never come up with anything as useless as golf." It was true. We golf every day, walking the course. It's an escape from music, a way to clear your mind and get some exercise.

Beth came back from the ladies room. She was perfect. A petite blonde, perfect face and tiny perky boobs. She couldn't weigh more than one hundred pounds. You just had to hate her but you couldn't, she was fragile.

"God! The ladies room is disgusting, looks like a bomb hit it." said Beth

“I went in there and there was no toilet paper.” said Stephanie.

“I went in there and some dude with a skirt on had the toilet seat up and was pissing in there.” I added.

We all laughed. It was pretty disgusting. Ladies rooms were to be avoided as much as possible during gigs because they inevitability got fucked up by drunk people during the course of the night. If you had to pee, do it early. The later you waited the more likely you were to catch a disease, see something you wished you hadn’t or walk in on a stink bomb from hell or worse!

Chapter 2

A new gig in a new joint. The other band wives weren’t joining me tonight, so it would mean a night of boredom and aloneness, no girl talk.

I thought about Stephanie’s problem. Sex was a tricky issue. You never really knew the mechanics of the problem unless you were there in the room and trying to imagine it was even worse. I couldn’t even try.

Our sex life was pretty good, in a regular, predictable sort of way. There were no kinky surprises or weird encounters, just the usual late Sunday morning routine. Safe yet satisfying. Phil was pretty much on schedule with his desire. (Or lack of it)

We had a lot of passion in the beginning of our relationship. Our heated arguments would often end up in a lovemaking session in the kitchen or on the floor. Now if we argued we'd end up on our computers, endlessly Googling crap or searching EBay for more useless junk. EBay has probably saved a lot of marriages.

I don't know much about Jon and Beth's private life. Beth kept a tight lid on that relationship. I knew they had some problems but I kept out of it. They had issues, but were quiet about it.

The band was setting up at The Surf Café, a cool little known joint by the railroad tracks. You could watch the trains go by from bamboo window shades. Phil was setting up his drum set. It was a pink champagne set he had from when he was a kid. Phil keeps all his equipment in pristine condition. Ian was on his knees, rummaging through a bag of cords. Jon was walking around in an aimless, dazed stupor, carrying his beer in one hand and smoking a cig with another.

Phil comes over for some customary hooch out of my bag. He is almost out; the Captain Morgan rum bottle is getting empty. I sit at a high top table by the window, trying to stay out of the way. The band is always tense when setting up their shit. Must be a macho thing, testosterone pumping through their veins as they check the mics and amplifiers.

No girl talk tonight, this sucks…I miss the gossip, the friendly banter, the endless complaining and moaning. I knew Stephanie was at home, but where was Beth tonight?

"Where's Beth?" I asked Jon

"Rehab." He said quietly.

"No way." I was shocked.

"Yeah, she freaked out last night, almost killed herself…Again." He looked sad for his age.

"Oh my God….I am so sorry." I put my arm around Jon. He was such a good kid.

"Yeah, me too," he said.

I felt really bad for Jon. This was like the fifth time that Beth had relapsed. He loved her, so he kept on hanging on, hoping she could get it together. But then she'd freak out if something went wrong, and drink herself into a state of hysteria. Jon was cute, real skinny and bony and tall. He looked like a duckling that was yet to turn into a swan. He had long brown hair and about five days worth of beard on his face.

"So what now?" I asked.

"I don't know, just take it day by day I guess."

I nodded and smiled at him in a reassuring way. He went to the bar to get another beer. That couple had drama all the time. We didn't really have that kind of drama any more, we were getting mellow in our old age.

I looked around the bar. Two blondes came in, some dudes were at the bar watching the game on the big Plasma above the bar. It would be a good night. Jon had a lot of original songs he did. He was a really good songwriter.

Phil was trying to help him get his shit to some important ears in the industry. Phil considered himself a mentor to Jon. Jon considered himself the next best thing in the music business. He was pretty confident of his abilities. But Jon's' downfall was that he was stubborn and wanted to produce himself. Phil disagreed. Phil wanted to talk him into doing a record with great session players on it, a masterpiece to be his calling card.

Jon was talking about maybe moving out to Austin,Texas to be a player in a bigger market. He would be playing with the big boys out there. Phil didn't think he was ready yet. Phil said give it another year, but Jon was fired up and ready to haul ass. If he didn't have the girl holding him back he probably would have left already.

I sipped my soda. Today had been a shitty day at work. Why was it that there is always some controlling bitch at work that wants to put her power trip on you? First she comes off as a friend, a confidant and then turns all the info that she has gleaned on me into ammunition for her power play. She confronted me today but I backed off and ignored her. The anger was still lingering inside of me. I try not to be too stressed because I have heard that stress can cause cancer. I'm not getting cancer because of this woman at work!!!

I tried to forget about it all. This was our music world, a world separate from the real world of bosses and paychecks and fax machines and the bullshit called the day job. The guys did not have day jobs. They were artists. Someone had to keep the bills paid and do the boring stuff.

This was the night shift. This is our time to create and make music and hang out and be cool. I tried to forget it, let it all go…Just be cool baby, be cool…

Ian and Jon came over to my table and started talking shit about the band Greenday. Phil tested the mics, bathed in pink and blue lights. It was going to be a long night, without the girls…

Stephanie ran the bath water and put in some bubble bath. The bubbles reached to the rim of the tub. She put her finger in. The water was the perfect temperature. She took off her robe and looked at herself in the mirror. She was well rounded, her breasts were full and her behind voluptuous. She didn't feel bad about her body, not as bad as Ian did. When she was alone she was totally comfortable in her nakedness. Around him she was self-conscious and always felt as though she had to live up to some porn star fantasy or something. Didn't he know those women were all airbrushed?

She sat back in the tub and lit an aromatherapy candle, Hawaiian Dream. It did smell heavenly. It felt so good to be home, alone, to unwind and relax. She didn't really feel like hanging out in some crowded, loud bar again, although it was always nice to be near Ian when he was playing. But she needed this alone time. They were always running around to his band practices, work gigs and rehearsals.

Her mind wandered to Brad. He was her secret soul mate. She wondered what he was doing right now. Maybe he was thinking of her too. She had checked him out on Face Book. He was there, along with his wife and three kids. She often thought of him.

She and Brad had shared an out of body connection once. It was like two souls coming together, it was more than physical, it was spiritual. He was like no other man she had ever known.

But she knew that the minute she met Ian he was the one for her. She just knew. She wanted more than anything in the world just to please him.

Stephanie lay back in the tub and astral projected to Brad's bed in Nantucket. She could imagine lying there and he would be making love to her and loving her body, mind and soul.

Her cell phone rang. She looked at the number. It was Ian.

"Hello."

"Hi baby, you sound kind of tired. Are you alright?" he asked.

"Yeah, I'm fine…How's the gig?" she asked

"We haven't started yet…..I was just thinking of you."

"Really cool…I was just thinking of you too." It was true.

"What are you doing now?' he asked.

"I'm in the tub."

"I have to go…We're going on, I'll talk to you later baby."

She hung up the phone and astral traveled back to Nantucket.

The lights in the joint dimmed down. The band kicked into the first song, an original called "You." Jon was electric on his guitar, moving and grooving to the rhythm. Phil was steady on the drums and Ian was mellow on bass. The band sounded really good.

Beth lay in her hospital bed and stared at the TV mounted on the wall. She was in here because she had fucked up once again. Tears rolled down her cheeks. Why? Why was she so fucked up? Was it because of her mother? Because of Jon? Because of her? Who was to blame? It seemed as though everyone in her life tried to control her every move. She felt trapped and alone. She wondered where Jon was tonight. Was he with someone else?

Jon sang on stage, bright lights shining in his eyes. He had to fight back the urge to cry as he sang Beth's song. The song he wrote for her. The song he was sure would be a number one hit all over the world if only the world could hear his music. Every word resonated in his heart. He thought of Beth locked up somewhere, alone in some ward. It tore him apart. He was unable to reach out to her, to hold her and tell her it would all be all right.

Beth picked up the phone. She dialed Jon's number. It rang and rang and then his voicemail picked up. She hung up. Fuck it. She knew he was getting tired of her. But she loved him so much. Why couldn't she just keep it together? Why? Why?

Stephanie stepped out of the tub and grabbed her white terry cloth robe and wrapped her wet hair up in a towel. She rubbed some almond cream on her face. She loved beauty products, they made her feel so pampered.

She once again thought of Brad. Why did these feelings persist after so many years? She sat down at her laptop and looked at his picture again on Face Book. There he was, smiling and looking as handsome as ever. She thought of sending him a message but changed her mind. If he still cared for her he would have to make the first move. Why should she?

Ian would be home later. She had to try with Ian. She would lay awake in the dark, waiting for him. Maybe tonight he would come home and they would make love, maybe…unless he was too damn tired, his usual excuse.

The band decided what to play. They counted down the song…2,3,4…it was a song I've heard so many times before, a cover song. I watched Phil. He waved to me. Things were going well tonight, we hadn't had an argument yet, which was a miracle. He usually would find a way to say some nasty quip and piss me off by the end of the night.

The clock read 3:25am. Stephanie lay in bed and pretended to be asleep. She heard the door open. Ian was home. She lay naked on the bed, her body bathed in the moonlight. He stumbled into the bedroom.

"Hi."

"You awake?"

"Yeah, I've been waiting for you."

"Why baby?"

"You know, I thought that maybe we might…"

"Uh….I don't feel well…." He threw up on the bed.

Chapter 3

Beth was checking out of the hospital. Her mom was there, waiting for her. They walked down the long, white, thickly carpeted corridor together.

"Got all your stuff?" she said nervously, toying with her cell phone.

"Yes Mom." she sighed.

They walked to the parking lot. Beth clutched her overnight bag, which was full of her stuff she needed for her stay. Shampoo hairbrush, underwear and a signed CD of Jon's. They were "her" songs. She knew he had written them for her. She was his inspiration, his muse.

Beth would call him as soon as she was out of her mother's earshot. Her mother had it out for Jon, she feared for his safety around her mother. She could be vicious. They drove in silence for a while, past the pain clinics and parking lots and strip malls. Finally her mother spoke. Here it comes, she thought.

"I hope this was the last time." She said sternly and quietly.

"Yes Mom." she rolled her eyes.

"Why do you behave this way?" she persisted.

"Oh God Mom, don't start on me now…."

"I just want the best for you. Can't you see that?" her tone was moving into a high nasal pitch.

"I know…. It'll be all right. I swear. It's just me….It's just me…"

"Ok, please leave Jon alone. I don't want you seeing that boy." Her fingers fumbled with her cigarette.

“He’s not a boy Mom, he’s a man and I am not a girl anymore. I am a woman.” she said defiantly.

“He’s bad for you honey, he upsets you….Look at what has happened to you.”

“No Mom… He doesn’t…. It’s not his fault that I freaked out. It’s my fault, all my fault. Why can’t you understand it had nothing to do with him? It’s me! It’s just me…..”

“Heed my warning child.”

“Mom!!!!!!…”

“Let him come to you.” She exhaled.

Beth sulked back in her seat. Here was her wonderful mother controlling her life again. Why didn’t she just leave them alone? Beth made up her mind. She would run away with Jon, far, far away and they would start their life together somewhere new. They would live on an island surrounded by coconut trees and eat pineapples and live in a grass hut. He would catch fish and she would cook over a fire.

Her mother clung to her because Dad had left them five years ago. Her mother was overprotective, demanding, controlling and impossible. Most of her friend’s mothers were really cool, but hers wasn’t. She was a control freak.

Stephanie turned on the Zumba video. The music started to play and a Barbie doll instructor gave orders. Step 1, step 2, back, back, step to the side…. She played the tape for forty-five minutes and then collapsed on the sofa in a heap of sweat.

Stephanie was determined to be skinny. If this was what Ian wanted then this was what he was going to get. She was willing it to happen. She wanted the pounds of fat to melt off her body until you could see bones, ribs and muscle. She was very muscular from years of running. Somewhere under this body was her dream body and she would get to it.

Stephanie knew why she was eating. It had to do with her past. Her parents had been very abusive to her growing up. She didn't trust people anymore. She only trusted Ian. He would never hurt her. And she trusted food. Food provided the comfort she carved, the acceptance…Food didn't betray you and connive behind your back or humiliate you or call you stupid. Food was nice. It was safe. She thought back to all the horrendous things her mother had done to her. And her father too. Her mother was an actress and her father was just a bum. An alcoholic and a drug addict. She didn't even know if her father was alive or dead. He might be dead on the street somewhere. Her dear father had left her for two weeks on the sofa with a hundred and five degree temperature and her mother had just allowed it. She hated them, she was glad she was away from them all now. Now her challenge was to be thin and show them all she could be a winner. She had to win. She had to…She would.

Chapter 4

The announcement hit the band like a bomb. Jon was going to Texas. It was a done deal, he'd be leaving Monday. Phil was crushed. Jon was his friend, he loved playing in the band and he wasn't sure if Texas was the answer to Jon's' dreams. But it was worth a try, he had to admit.

Jon was young, had no ties and it was official that he and Beth were breaking up, he couldn't handle any more of her drama. I was neutral on the situation. Of course I wanted the band to stay together but couldn't deny that maybe Jon was better off in a bigger town, a town of guitar gun slingers and music agents on the prowl who were sure to see his talent and turn him into a mega star or demi guitar God. Did he have what it took? Time would tell.

I called Beth to see how she was doing. The phone rang twice and she picked up.

"Hello?" she said

"Hi Beth, its me, Heather."

"Oh, hi…." She sounded sleepy.

"Sorry, did I wake you?"

"No, it's this medicine I'm on makes me tired. I guess it's an anit-depressant."

"We were so worried about you."

"I know. I'm an idiot."

"No, you're not…We understand."

"Jon's leaving." She said bluntly.

"Yeah, I heard about that."

"Well, screw him because I'm leaving too."

"You're going with him?"

"No, I'm moving to Brooklyn."she said matter of factly.

"Brooklyn?" I was surprised.

"I heard it's really way cool there. I want a fresh start, you know, no memories of the times we had together and all that shit. I need to get away."

"Yeah, I can totally understand that…Are you sure you feel up to it?"

"Yes, I have got to get away from my mother, she is killing me."

"Wow, alright. I am behind you if you need anything…You know you can always call me."

“Thanks girlfriend. I will miss you.”

“Yes, we’ll all miss you too……Let’s have coffee before you take off, alright?”

“Alright.”

I hung up the phone. She was so fragile and then all this strength, strength to leave her home and run off to Brooklyn, away from her friends and family and Jon. I wonder if he knew yet. Of course he knew. I guess he was the first person she had told. Kids. They sure were crazy. Not like us old folks, all set in our ways, dinner at seven, chicken and mashed potatoes and green beans. It was so predictable and yet so comforting to be on our own little schedule outside from the madness in the world.

I went to the back room where Phil kept all his paraphernalia and rummaged through some boxes. I came across and old book of mine I had bought on the Internet. It was called, “ The Food Of Santa Fe.” I had forgotten how much I loved this book. It had beautiful color pictures of authentic recipes from the American Southwest. Dishes like Lobster Ceviche with Plantain Chips and Grilled Swordfish Tacos.

I would love to escape South Florida with Phil one day and head to Santa Fe. I could just imagine staying in a quaint little bed and breakfast, waking up to fresh coffee and croissants and spending the day rummaging through art galleries and antique shops, taking in all the fabulous art and native pottery and sculpture. Would Phil be into it? Highly unlikely. But it was one of my desires. There were things I wanted to do in life, places I wanted to see that had nothing to do with Phil. I walked into the living room where he was intonating an old guitar of his.

"Are you finished with that thing yet?" I asked.

"Nope. Do you like these stickers?" he pointed to a bunch of ratty stickers.

"I like the one with the Mickey Mouse on it."

"Yeah, I like that one too." He pressed it onto a drum.

"I talked to Beth, she's moving to Brooklyn."

"Really? Why? She planning on jumping off the Brooklyn Bridge? Ha, ha…."

I hit him.

"You're an asshole!" He ducked, protecting his guitar.

"Don't touch my guitar, you'll hurt it. You destroyer."

"I'm going to start dinner."

"Good because I am hungry. I haven't eaten a thing all day. There's no food in this house." He complained

“What about the cereal this morning and the wrap from Wendy’s this afternoon?”

“Ah, that’s nothing…..” What a moaner, he was always snacking. The man could eat constantly.

“Alright, call me if you need me….”

Stephanie stepped out of the patio door into the garden. She loved her garden and had planted a vegetable garden there. Her favorite vegetables were all there, tomatoes, corn, squash, cucumber, watermelons, carrots, basil and green beans. It felt good to be eating natural, she felt it was better for her allergies and diabetes. Ian had helped, digging the garden and planting all the seeds for her. She felt so lucky. A strawberry plant was even starting to bloom. She felt so proud.

She went over to the little cage where she kept her two angels. Pumpkin and Muffin. They were two of the cutest little bunnies she had ever seen and she loved them to pieces. She cut a carrot and gave it to Pumpkin. He munched it hungrily. These were her babies…..

She felt good today, despite her allergy attack last night. She didn’t know what had set it off, but it had put her out, wheezing and panting for air. Ian had been out playing a gig so she was home alone. She felt like calling an ambulance but then the claustrophobic feeling went away and she had fallen asleep on the sofa, in front of the TV with her inhaler at her side.

Ian was out all the time these days She didn't always go with him to his gigs because she was just so damn tired all the time from her job as a receptionist. She dreamed that one day she would have her own business designing designer handbags but that seemed like a far away dream, a distant goal that was somehow unattainable. She would work towards her dream one small baby step at a time….Like the weight. One pound at a time…..

We met Jon Monday morning in the Publix parking lot. Phil wanted to buy an old pedal from him to give him some cash for the trip. Jon looked excited and seemed anxious to get going. We did the pedal deal and Phil gave Jon $100.00 bucks. We hoped it would help him on his journey. A man had to eat on the road, buy gas and sleep somewhere all that cost money, a commodity which Jon was short of at the moment.

"Thanks guys…I'll call you."

"For sure, we're here if you need anything…."

We all hugged and Jon got into his black pickup truck and drove off towards the highway. For a minute I thought that Phil was going to cry or something. But he didn't. I guess Phil felt a fatherly sentiment about Jon.

"He'll be back soon, I'm sure." I said reassuringly.

"Yeah. I'm not convinced that Austin is the answer for him. I am going to try to get his songs to my buddy in Nashville, they'll appreciate his songwriting up there. I doubt those hillbilly's in Texas will dig his tunes."

"We'll see."

I wanted to be optimistic for Jon's sake. But I was beginning to wonder if he was making the right move. So our band was over….Now what? Do we try to replace Jon with another guitar player?

Almost as if reading my thoughts Phil said, "I guess I might look for a replacement for Jon. I know a few guys. Nobody as special as him though. Talent like that only comes around once in awhile."

Time would tell.

Chapter 5

Beth stared at her closet. It was bulging with clothes, shoes, handbags and other stuff that she had crammed in there. What a mess! How to determine what to pack was becoming a big chore.

Of course her mother had flipped out when she told her she was moving to Brooklyn. But this was it. She had to move on with her life. She was twenty-five and tired of being treated like a coddled teenager.

Her friend Mike had called her to tell her that he was moving to Brooklyn too. An odd co-incidence, she thought. He liked her, he had always followed her around, sent her flowers, showed up at her doorstep. He was sort of a stalker in a safe way. She knew him and his family, his brother was friends with Jon, she wasn't really totally creeped out by him but he was sort of weird. She hoped he wouldn't become a problem in Brooklyn, where she intended to start her life over and remake herself, become a working girl in New York City, get a job, have a career, be serious and stop all the drama that she felt with Jon.

She loved Jon, almost to his very soul. She felt that they were soul mates, she had thought that they would have started a family together, bought a place and started their life. But his music was his life, she had come to know. She was second, music was first. He would never be the husband she was looking for. But part of her wanted him to be the one so much, the thought of living without him was what cause her to go off the edge, to try to end it all, to end the pain.

She packed up her suitcase with some clothes, threw some sweaters in there and some shoes. Her trusty old bear Freddy was on her bed, she threw him in there too, just in case she needed a friend in her bed late at night. He would keep her safe, she knew it.

Her mother knocked on the door.

“Come in” she said

“Hi…How’s your packing going?”

“It’s ok…I threw in Freddy.”

“A good idea…he’s been with you all your life. He’s a good friend. You can trust him.”

“Yeah Mom…”
Here it comes, she’s going to lecture me now, tell me I am making a mistake….Instead her mother handed her an envelope.

“I have this for you. Open it.” Her Mom handed her the thick white envelope. She opened it up. It was full of old, sweet smelling money.

“Mom?” she said in disbelief.

“I saved it for you…. I know you will need it.”

She threw her arms around her mother and kissed her neck. “Oh thank you Mom…I don’t know what to say.”

“Just use it wisely honey.”

“I will Mom, thank you.” The tears started to roll down her cheeks and soon she was sobbing. “I’m so sorry for all the trouble I have caused you.” She blubbered.

Her mother hugged her tightly. “It’s all right honey, it’s all right….”

She wiped her nose on her sleeve.

“How about some tea?” her Mom said.

“Ok.”

Jon checked his watch. He would be due in Jacksonville any time soon. The plan was he would stay with his buddy Paul and then drive the rest of the way tomorrow at dawn. Being on the road sure gave a man time to think. He thought about all the friends and family he had left behind. He thought about his girl. He didn’t know how he felt, it was like his insides were all torn up. He wanted to make it, he knew he had to break away, to be seen and heard somewhere far away from home.

He called Phil on his cell. “I’m in Jacksonville man.”

“No shit? Already?”

“Yeah, time just flies when you’re having fun.”

“We miss ya already man.”

“I’ll be back, just don’t know when……” his voice trailed off slightly shaking.

“I like your pedal.”

“It was a steal…”

“It’s going right on EBay.”

“I’ll bet it is.”

“I’m sure I’ll double my money.”

“You always do you cheap fucker.”

“I love when you compliment me.”

“It’s my pleasure.”

“Alright, say hi to the cornpones in Texas for me.”

“I will…..”

“Talk to you later dude.”

We were home, in for the evening. Phil was watching TV in the living room, some Western or something. Some annoying film I wouldn’t watch if you paid me to. I find when cowboys and Indians are involved I can pass on it unless Robert Redford is in it. Phil was concerned for Jon being on the road. There were some wildfires that had sprung up in Texas and over four hundred and fifty homes had already been destroyed. He was worried that his pal might run into some trouble.

I was busy on the computer, scouting out publishers for my children's book. I had the story written, but no illustrations. There seemed to be hundreds of so-called vanity publishers, people that took your book and your money. I had to watch out for these scams.

It was good to be home for a change. Usually we were out at some bar, loud noise, music, drinking and drunk people. Home was quiet. We could concentrate on the cat and relax for a change. I didn't mind being home at all.

I made myself a nice, hot cup of tea. My favorite tea was English breakfast. I loved the deep, rich taste of it. I grew up on Red Rose teabags, with the little figurines inside. I did enjoy a hot tea while cruising the net.

The phone rang in the other room. I could hear Phil's voice rise. What was he talking about? I tried to listen but only caught tidbits of his conversation. Phil came in the room.

"It's Jon…" he said, looking worried

"What is it?"

“He’s been in an accident.”

I froze in my chair. “Oh my god! Is he alright?’

“Yeah, he’s okay but his car is totaled…. Some woman hit him. She’s blaming him though, making it out to be his fault. She was drunk.”

“Jeez!”

“He’s got insurance.”

“Thank God for that.”

“He’s coming home.”

“Really?”

“Yup. He doesn’t like it out there.”

“I don’t blame him…..”

“I am kind of disappointed though.”

‘Why?”

“I thought he would stick it out, try to make it big. I had high hopes for the kid..”

“Hey honey, sometimes that’s not how it goes, sometimes you do what’s best for you at that time in your life.”

"I know. I know. Glad he's alright." He sighed.

So Jon was coming back. The band was back together again. Only now Beth was gone. And she wouldn't be coming back…Or would she?

Stephanie sat at a table at The Olive Garden. She looked around. It was a Tuesday afternoon; around 4pm. Nobody she knew would ever see her here. She ordered the Never-Ending Pasta Bowl and a diet Coke. She turned on her Blackberry Playbook and went to Face Book. She clicked on his picture. There he was…Her soul mate. She read a few of his posts, mostly boring stuff. She looked at the pictures of his wife and his kids.

She felt evil, like some evil home wrecker that was about to commit a terrible, terrible sin. She did it…. She pressed the private message button. She could not believe she was doing this. It was the sneakiest, most lowly thing she could do and yet there was no stopping her.

She wrote. "Hi Brad. It's me, Stephanie. I have been thinking about you and hope that you are fine and happy. I miss you. I would like to hear from you and catch up on old times. Steph."

That wasn't so bad, she wasn't wrecking any home. She was just catching up on an old friend. An old friend she yearned for with every fiber of her body. She wondered what he would think of her if he saw her. Would he still desire her? Would their feelings still be as intense as they had been? Or was it all in her mind?

Her Never-Ending Pasta Bowl arrived and she dug in. Food. Her friend. Food that always accepted her and kept her from loneliness. She would diet tomorrow. Right now she was way too stressed to not eat. She needed the caloric intake.

Chapter 6

Beth boarded the plane holding her carry on bag in one hand and he cell phone with another. She was waiting for Jon's' call. He knew today was her flight to New York. Just as she was sliding into her window seat the phone rang. It was him.

"Hi" he said

"Hey! I didn't think you were going to call me." she lied.

"Why?"

"I don't know, but I'm glad that you did….I thought we broke up."

"I came back from Austin."

"You did?" She was shocked.

"Yeah, I'm back. I didn't dig it out there too much. Too many cowboys I guess." He failed to mention the accident.

"Wow!!."

"So, you're on the plane huh?"

"Yeah. We're about to take off."

"Any cute guys next you?"

"No, just some old man eating an egg sandwich."

"Lucky you….Lucky him"

"Yeah….I'm just so fucking lucky."

Tear started to roll down her cheeks. She blubbered into the phone.

"Jon, I'm so sorry for everything." She whispered into the phone.

He was crying too, at the other end of the phone.

“Yeah, me too. I feel like it’s my fault. I really love you still. It’s just really hard for me to deal with your problems, you know?”

Silence.

“Yeah, well, maybe you can come and visit me.”

“Yeah, okay. I will, one you get settled into your new place. Alright?”

“Alright.” She wiped her nose on her sleeve. “The plane is taking off, I have to go.”

“Bye”.

“Bye”.

The plane took off and Beth stared out the window. The buildings and cars and houses all got smaller and smaller and she cried a little. The flight attendant came around with a drink cart and a headphone set.

“Would you care for anything Miss?’

“Yes, I’ll take a vodka on the rocks please.”

She needed this last drink. She needed it bad. For the first time in a long time she suddenly felt grown up. She wanted to forget the pain, all the pain she felt and let the world slip away. She was going to make her own decisions now.

There would be no one to blame but herself. Her life was changing. She was going to take control of her life.

It was a quiet Sunday afternoon and Phil was doing his usual, watching the game on TV. I was busy organizing our clothes and doing laundry at the same time. Things seemed peaceful. I thought about the band. It was good that Jon was back, now things would get back to normal again. I thought about Beth, all alone in Brooklyn.

I was lucky, I thought, to have a stable relationship. Oh sure, we had our nitpicky fights and squabbles, sometimes a major blowout when I would threaten to leave, but we always made up quickly and life was back to normal again. I must have threatened to leave one hundred times. Phil never once said he would leave. Never.

I couldn't imagine life without Phil. He was a huge part of me, sometimes I didn't know where one of us stopped and the other one began. I knew all his jokes, his history, his showbiz career. I knew his many moods. His hungry mood, his leave me alone now moods, his EBay mood, his don't fuck with me now mood. And he knew mine. Most of the time.

Sometimes I would slip into the past and try to deal with things that have happened to me, ugly things that I would never tell him. But those were times gone by. They just lingered a bit and he would wonder why I was pissed off.

He had no idea it had nothing to do with him or us, just shit that happened by jerks a log time ago. They seemed so unimportant now. I wondered why they still lingered in my memory. It's hard to totally erase the past.

He knew if I was caught in a little white lie, he knew if I was late, he knew if I was over-eating or hiding something. It was actually kind of sickening knowing someone so well. But that was it, we knew each other after fourteen years together.

"Baby, get me some more soda." He cried from the armchair.

"Ok."

What was he? Too helpless to get it himself ? I poured him some soda. There was a postcard from Jon on the fridge. It said, "Music is life. Jon"

I thought about Jon and his intense drive to be a musician. It seemed like it was the most important thing in his life. But what would happen once life stepped in and threw him some obstacles like a wife and snot nosed kids? Would music still come first? Or would his priorities change? I knew he was dreaming big time, Grammys and limousines and gold records. What would happen if he had to become a manager at an auto parts store? I hoped that his dream would happen for him before it got too late.

I handed Phil the soda and kissed him on his head.

“Thanks baby,” he said absent-mindedly.

I went back to folding laundry. Sometimes even a boring day was satisfying.

Chapter 7

The guys were gigging again, tonight at an Irish bar. It was Jon’s’ first night out again since his comeback, so everyone was in an upbeat mood. Stephanie was sitting with me, in a large wooden banquette covered in green leather, chatting away about her day while browsing websites on her Blackberry Playbook. The guys sounded good tonight, they were pretty much in sync.

I glanced over at Phil and blew him a kiss. He smiled but had a focused look on his face. His playing was intense. Ian was onstage, smiling and looking pretty careless. Stephanie and I were deep in conversation about buying houses, her allergies, our obsession with aromatherapy. There was so much to talk about. We were still both wondering about Beth but no information had escaped Jon’s lips, not yet. We would be sure to get the scoop eventually. The music was so loud I was convinced that I was going deaf.

Something in me was restless tonight. I felt a longing to run away from my humdrum life. I had been fantasizing about far away places like Africa and Bora Bora and Thailand. Anywhere but here in dullsville, living my dull and predictable life. I guess part of me loved the dull life and part of me loathed it. I often told myself I should run away and do something exotic. But I never did. I just sort of plodded along. In my world even changing my brand of toothpaste was exciting. Something to Twitter about anyhow. I Tweeted the most useless tidbits of information to complete strangers. That's what my life was coming down to. I have turned into a social media geek.

I could visualize my humble tiki hut home close to an ocean, with bamboo-covered floors and a modern kitchen and a bedroom with a four-poster bed with mosquito netting around it. I wanted to live that dream. If only to escape reality for just a little while. The table jolted and Stephanie grabbed her handbag.

" I need my inhaler!" Stephanie gasped. Her face turned a deep red and her chest was heaving up and down.

I sprang back to life and watched as she almost choked, wheezing and huffing and puffing. Stephanie's' allergies were acting up tonight. Must be the dust or the alcohol or the mold in the ceiling.

"You feeling better now?" I asked

"Yes."

"That sucks."

“I hate it…I have to go to the doctor soon and get shots.”

“That sucks. I am glad that you feel better.”

We sat in silence awhile and just listened to the band.

“It’s so weird without Beth huh?” Stephanie said

“Yeah, I was just thinking the same thing. Have you heard anything?”

“No.”

We didn’t know how Beth was doing. No one had heard from her. I was wondering if she could get her life back together again. Maybe her and Jon would get back together. They were both so young and so in love time would tell. Meanwhile Jon had a lot of young, willing and able chicks that dug him. One chick in particular kept prancing around in front of the band in her short shorts……Jeez, did these women have any morals? The guys didn’t care. They loved it.

Jon played guitar like a menacing God. The crowd was awed. I looked around at the chairs and tables, the stained glass ceiling and at the flickering TV screens on the walls. The place was jammed with thirsty patrons out for a good time.

Someone tapped me on the shoulder. It was Patrick, the guitar player from the band next door. I guess he had come over to check out his competition.

"Band sounds good except for the crappy drummer." He said jokingly.

I laughed. Patrick was a wild man but seemed really impressed by our boys, evilly watching them with a slightly jealous stare.

The band laid into, "Voodoo Child" by Hendrix, with a long, screaming solo and nonstop drums and bass. The band was really pumped up after being apart from each other. Jon was rocking it out, singing his heart out.

The night went by talking our girl talk and hanging out with our guys on break. I felt somewhat detached from it all and Phil was ignoring me. I felt a bit unloved and neglected. But I wanted him to have his band time with the guys. I wasn't so important. I ordered some fries, mostly to relieve the boredom.

"You shouldn't be eating this late." Phil finally noticed me now that I was eating.

"I'm hungry."

"You're not serious about losing weight are you?" he persisted.

Oh God, here we go again, more nagging. Nag, nag, nag.

There was a bit of change in the air tonight. Later that afternoon I had slipped Jon a number for a Nashville producer. Jon was as broke as a flea on a camels back. He needed money. He needed fame. He needed to get the hell out of this town…

I was looking forward to getting home to peace and quiet. But it would be hours before the guys would pack up. There was the job of getting paid, getting rebooked, packing up the gear, talking about shit and more shit, having one last shot or beer and counting and dividing the tips…..I knew the drill only too well. Music wafted around me. I'd love to be home in bed now, my head buried in the soft pillow, away from noise….

Beth sat in the back of the cab watching the Brooklyn streets. There were storefronts going by and rows of brownstones. Korean grocers and Laundromats lit the night on every corner. It stared to rain violently. The rain was beating down on the windshield. The cabbie pulled over in front of a large brownstone and stopped the meter.

"This is it Miss. That'll be twenty-five."

She paid him and slipped him a five-dollar tip. So this was it, her new home. She ran out of the cab, getting soaked.

There was a mailbox by the door. She turned the key and dragged her suitcase inside. There was a flight of stairs ahead of her. The cabbie jumped in the foyer.

“Let me help you.” He picked up her suitcase and bound up the stairs with amazing strength.

“Thank you so much.”

“Take care Miss.”

Beth turned the key in the door. It opened slowly. She stepped inside and switched on the light and took her first glimpse of her new apartment. The place was a light airy studio with wooden floors. A white paper lantern hung from the ceiling. The walls were painted linen white and there was a quaint fireplace in the living room. She went to the window and looked out. The city lights were dazzling. She had a home now. This was the beginning. Her landlord had ordered her a futon and she plopped down. She felt alone and excited at the same time. This was her new life. Her own new life.

She went downstairs to the Korean grocery store down the block. The rain had stopped now and the streets were damp and smelled of wet, fresh concrete. Some young guys gave her the eye in the store. She didn’t stare back. She helped herself to the salad bar, filling up a plastic container of food and vegetables. The little old Korean lady behind the counter smiled at her.

"You new here? I never seen you before girl?"

"Yes."

"Ah good....You very, very pretty.... Now I have another customer. You come see me, my name Lucy."

"Ok thanks Lucy...I'm Beth."

As she was heading out of the store Mike brushed by her. The stalker.

"Hey! What a fucking co-incidence!" he said.

"Mike?"

"Yup. I just moved in the neighborhood Beth. Looks like we'll be neighbors now."

"Yeah....Cool." Mike definitely spooked her out.

"I heard about you and Jon. That's tough babe."

"Yeah. I'll be alright."

"See ya around."

"Bye....."

She took her food up to the apartment. She ate, and thought of Jon. What was he doing now? She wondered.

Was he thinking of her? She doubted it. She was probably the last thing on his mind. She tried to not think about her time in the hospital. That had to be a thing of the past. No more fuck ups in this new life. Tomorrow she would see about a job in the city. She had an interview at nine am. Time to get some rest.

Chapter 8

The sound check was deafening. Drums that sounded like pounding sledgehammers, a guitar that screamed and bass that thumped oozed into my soul. Something was ringing in the PA, the guys had yet to detect the problem. Jon adjusted the PA. The ringing stopped. Tonight was a rainy and quiet night. I doubted that the crowds would be out on the avenue, but the band was optimistic.

I was sitting alone in a large wooden booth, discretely going over my bills. I had more bills than money to pay bills. I was starting to wonder which credit card would be the first to slide. I hated to ruin my credit, but it was getting pretty desperate in my poverty.

Ian was setting up his bass amp. I asked him about Stephanie and he said she wasn't coming tonight, too bad, no girl talk for me. I was stuck with the guys tonight. Somebody had ordered sweet potato fries and they arrived steaming in a green and white basket. It was going to be a long night.

Stephanie poured the boiling water into her teacup. This was her favorite blend of Earl Grey English Breakfast tea. She needed a good cup to relax while she perused the Internet. Her cat Sabrina was acting up tonight. She bent down to pet her but the cat swatted her good with her paw, cutting her skin.

"Sabrina!" she yelled, and the cat scampered out the sliding door.

She wiped up the cut with some alcohol. It was good to be home alone; maybe she would have a bath with some incense and bubbles. Maybe she would even get around to reading her new book. Stephanie checked out her email. Her cousin Katrina in North Carolina was getting married…She would have to send her a gift. She scrolled farther down. There it was, a message from Brad. She opened it up and held her breath anxiously.

It read:

Dear Stephanie,

What a wonderful surprise to hear from you. I am happy that you found a good guy to get married to. I found this out on Face Book. I also am married, as you probably know and we have two daughters. I have thought of you often, I hope that life is treating you well.... Thanks for being in touch, take care.

Best,

Brad

Hmmmn....So he was pretty much out of reach. He didn't love her anymore and was happily married... It hurt. She felt relieved that it was over for him. If only he knew how much she cared for him. He would have to remain a fantasy. She pushed him out of her mind. Men, what pricks they are, she thought.

She clicked on another website, her favorite designer of the moment Chloe Case. She loved the high fashion clothes, the whimsical shoes and the outrageous accessories.

She dreamed of designing a designer handbag and becoming rich and famous and her own boss. But it was just a dream. Right now she had to do one thing, lose weight and turn Ian on again. That was her number one priority. She dreamed of going from 210 to 130. She wanted a personal trainer to whip her into shape like on Oprah and The Biggest Loser. She had to exercise while Ian wasn't around. He only served to sabotage her efforts by feeding her French fries, cheese doodles and pretzels. She had to save her marriage.

Ian was good, busy in his bands and with his job. His goal was to become a valuable session player in Nashville. Nashville would be cool; she could see them there.

Stephanie pulled out some paper and began sketching some designs for the handbag. She couldn't really draw very well, but it was enough to get the idea across. A saddlebag style, stitching, a pouch for her secret scent. SB Creations, her initials. She had the whole game plan. Now to somehow put this into motion. Maybe one day she would be brave enough to approach Chloe Case with her idea in New York. Sure…what a dream that would be…She must be on acid or something.

Chapter 9

Beth caught the A train into the city. She was clad head to toe in black; her hair pulled into a chic ponytail and had on her new black patent leather boots.

All she had was an address scribbled on the back of a card. 500 Madison Avenue. She emerged at Grand Central Station and started walking. The harsh reality of daylight hit her and her feet pounded the pavement with the throngs of workers carrying Blackberries, wearing sneakers, juggling coffee cups and totting briefcases. 500 Madison Ave loomed large in front of her. It was a large, plain glass door. She pushed it open and went inside. The receptionist looked up at her from a granite desk.

“I’m here to see Ms Jenkins.”

“Oh yes, please take a seat. Your name?”

“Beth Polanski.”

“One moment….”

She sat and glanced around the office. There were Indian prints on the walls and a lively throw on the wooden floor. The office had some personality. She was curious about Melanie.

Melanie Jenkins was a prominent therapist in New York City. Beth had Googled her and found out that she graduated Magna Cum Laude from Yale University and had a sterling reputation. She wanted a job as an intern badly. This would get her foot in the door.

“Ms Jenkins will see you now.”

Beth followed the receptionist into the inner sanctum of the plush offices. Melanie was standing by the window watering a hanging plant.

“Ah Beth, sit down…Just watering Hazel, a gift from my mother. She loves ferns.”

They shook hands. Beth was surprised by how pretty Melanie was. She must have been around forty, with smooth skin and curly black hair.

"Welcome to New York." Said Melanie

"Thanks, I love it. It's so busy!"

"Yes, there is tremendous energy here. The city does take some getting used to…So, tell me about yourself."

"Well, I graduated FAU with a degree in Occupational Therapy."

"No, tell me about you." she said intensely.

"Well, I'm 24, I grew up in Florida. My father was a dentist and my mother is an artist. They are divorced. This is my first time living on my own and I love it. I plan to become very successful, much like yourself."

"Thank you. Well, let me get to the point. The position I have here is an intern position, as you know…. It involves handling patient's needs, running errands, keeping the office stocked up on supplies and being my personal assistant. Discretion is essential, of course…..I take great care to see that my personal life does not interfere with my professional life. Think it's the job for you?"

"Definitely."

"Ok then, you're hired. You can start next Monday at 9am. We'll just take it from there."

“Thank you Ms Jenkins.” She shook her hand.

“Just call me Melanie.”

Beth got up and smiled a big smile. Her adrenaline was pumping. She would have to call her mother to tell her the news, and Jon…Jon wasn’t her lover anymore. She felt a little down thinking about Jon. What was good news when you didn’t have someone to share it with?

She walked uptown to Central Park. The hot dog vendors were out, pigeons strolled the sidewalks and she felt excited to be alive. She was, in fact, very grateful that she was alive. Beth sat down on a park bench and watched the people stroll by. Life felt good.

Phil, Jon and Ian were tearing it up, playing some down and dirty slow blues. Phil was smiling at me. I was glad that he hadn’t dyed his beard bright red yet. I liked him the way he was, all gray hair.

The place was slow tonight. Jon was on center stage.

“There’s a red house over yonder, that’s where my baby stays.” He crooned.

I wondered about his Texas fiasco, too bad it hadn’t worked out for him. Maybe he would end up in Nashville with Ian one day. The future was as clear as mud.

I was thinking about a story I started to write. It was a children's story called Simon the Silly Snail. I've been writing children's stories for a while, I am self published which doesn't mean shit. I've thought of hiring an illustrator but don't have the money to do it quite yet. I'm just in the thinking stages, can't take myself too seriously as a writer.

I sat and listened to Jon singing one of Beth's songs. What did he think when he sang those songs? Did he think of her? Did it cause him pain? Did memories float through his mind? He was very mysterious.

I vowed to call Beth in Brooklyn and see how she was doing. Maybe one day us band wives would have a reunion. The night was droning on. I sat hunched in the booth surrounded by flickering media on big screen TV's, a blend of politics, sports and flashes of life from all over the world. My day was one day blending into the next.
Life and death, highs and lows, insanity and peace.

Chapter 10

Stephanie lay in bed tossing and turning. Something was bugging her and she just couldn't get it out of her mind. A dark, icky vibe washed over like a giant grizzly bear standing over her, jaws open, ready to attack.

She hopped out of bed and turned the light on. Her cell phone was flashing. A message. She checked the number. It was her mother. She had tracked her down again. Her mental mother was stalking her again, like she had done before. She'd stalked her brother and her uncle and now her, again.

Stephanie was freaking out. What if her mother was here at her house, watching her? Chills ran down her spine. She felt it was a matter of time before one day her mother would snap, go on a crazy killing spree and take her out.

It had been a few years sine she last heard from her. She remembered it well. She had suggested that they meet for coffee. She knew she hated coffee but she went. Her mother was sitting at the counter, a half dazed smile on her lips, sipping a cappuccino. She gave her no hug, no kiss , just a cold and vacant stare. She started bombarding her with questions about Ian. Why was she with him? Did he make enough money? When was she coming home to help her? She said she needed her, for what? Needed her to make her life more miserable again?

Stephanie shuddered art the thought that her mother had tracked her down again. She needed to get dressed go and meet Ian at the gig. It was only eleven. But she was paralyzed, terrified at the thought that maybe her mother was waiting for her outside in the dark. What if she was watching and waiting? She jumped under the covers and kept the lights on. Ian would be home soon....Tomorrow she was meeting up with her friend Candy for lunch. She would survive.

I sat and listened to the band. It was grooving tonight. Phil was doing well, despite his most recent bout of lactose intolerance. It seemed that just about everything he ate upset his stomach. French-fries, hamburgers, milk, all big no-nos, yet he continued to chow down his favorite foods. Meanwhile he toilet time was getting worse and worse, almost to the point of being unable to play on stage. I was getting scared for him.

I went to Whole Foods earlier in the week and looked around at the Gluten-Free department. Maybe that was the answer. I bought some crackers, some cereal and some pasta, all gluten free. Phil needed to take better care of that stomach of his....

He looked happy tonight playing with the band. Jon was looking excessively skinny in a tight white T-shirt and sagging pants that showed his yellow underwear. Ian was jamming away on bass. His face was swollen from having his wisdom teeth pulled, so he was playing with a kind of tortured precision.

The band was up for a cool gig in Sanibel Island. There was a fishing tournament there and we were booked to stay at the swanky Island Plantation resort. It would be great to get away from here for a while and mellow out in Sanibel.

I ordered a Coke and was sitting back watching the band when the door opened and in walked Beth. Jon was playing guitar and a look of disbelief washed over his face when he saw her. He kept on playing and a tiny, mysterious smile crept over his face.

Beth came over and I hugged her.

“Beth! What a surprise!”

“Yeah. I can’t believe I’m here.”

“You look great girl!”

“Thanks. I feel great.”

“How’s New York?”

“Great!”

The band took a break. Jon walked over to Beth with his arms outstretched.

“Babe!”

“I’m here….”

They hugged and kissed and I left them alone, I found Phil sitting on the side of the stage.

“Beth is back.” I said excitedly

“I see…” he said disapprovingly.

“So?”

“I smell trouble….” He said darkly.

“You are such a pessimist.”

‘We’ll see…”

“How’s your stomach?”

“Hurts a bit…I might have to go take another massive turd.”

“Spare me the details, ok?”

I gave him a kiss before he left and worried about him. I looked over at Beth and Jon, deep into each other. Wow. I thought, this was the happiest I’d seen Jon in ages, who always walked around in a sarcastic, cerebral tone of not caring. I guess they still loved each other.

It was already December 1st. the Thanksgiving holidays were over. We were all stuffed with turkey and cranberry and sweet potatoes and corn. Now the serious shopping would begin.

Phil had his list of items that he wanted, but what I had in mind was a golf course credit card that would let him play as much as he wanted. I knew he loved golf. So that was my dream gift for him. Whether I could afford it or not remained to be seen. I had already shopped on the internet for great stocking stuffers on Amazon, a golf glove, sunglasses, a CD…….Phil was a terrible child when It came to Christmas gifts and would squeeze and peek and try to figure out all his gifts.

I didn't know what I wanted, all I really needed was cash but nobody had any. In years past my bosses used to give me a cash bonus at the end of every year bit this too had dried up in the lousy economy. I guess I was lucky just to have a job. Yup. Times were tough. My credit cards were mounting up. Paying the minimum didn't get you very far out of debt. I wished I were financially secure. Wished I had like fifty grand in the bank, a little stash of cash….Maybe one day I would get there. Right now I had a long way to go.

Stephanie walked down Atlantic Avenue towards the Greenmarket. It was a perfect, sunny day, perfect to browse all the vendors that had their wares set up. She was thinking of her mother today. It had been a few weeks since the creepy call and nothing had come of it. She was beginning to feel a little foolish about being paranoid. Maybe her Mom would come around.

Things were going well with her and Ian. He was busy all the time and she had her own job to take care of, as well as her vegetable garden and her Zumba classes. Life was sweet.

She headed into the Greenmarket. There was a fish vendor there, with fresh Florida stone crabs on ice. Awesome!! There was a hot sauce lady there, selling her spicy hot sauces. She stopped at A Taste For Africa and ordered a chicken kabob. It looked so delicious on the grill, roasted and brown, covered in a BBQ sauce. She sat and ate. She felt so alive, so connected to the universe today. It was good to be out, to be free, to be young. She had her whole life ahead of her.

Ian had come around in the romance department. He brought her flowers for the first time in over a year and hugged her tight. She was flooded with emotion, happy that he wasn't taking her for granted. She felt if only she was skinnier he would pay her more mind. But that was coming. The inches were falling off her frame slowly. She was already one pants size smaller.

She had begun to sew her bag. She would sew at work when no one was looking, carefully lining up the edges of her design. The bag was almost done. She planned to submit it to Chloe Case in New York when it was complete. Her dream loomed ahead of her in full sail. She felt a power inside her that was unstoppable, a desire for revenge and success that enveloped her. She felt hungry and determined and was tired of being ignored. Soon they would pay attention to her when she walked into the room. Soon she would be a force to be reckoned with. Soon. When? She didn't know.

She sat and watched the people in the market. Their faces were so relaxed, they had their dogs and kids. She wished she could relax and be as peaceful and content with life. But she had to make her mark. She knew that deep down inside her was a powerful woman, a woman of strength and of substance. It was only a matter of time. Would Ian be able to stand the force? Would he wither? Would he stand behind her and be her man?

Time would tell.

Chapter 11

Phil was in his usual not so charming, fucked up mood as he loaded in his drums at Surf Café. The band was on again. Loading and unloading equipment seemed to be his biggest obstacle. This ritual took place before and after the intake of alcohol at every show in order to calm jittered nerves and anxiety about how the show was going to go.

At this point, I tried to stay out of the way of all oncoming disasters. It seemed no matter what I did nothing was ever right. It was very tiring and draining, all this energy wasted in stupid shit like dropping a bag of sticks or mishandling a snare drum. Very irritating stuff. I retreated to my corner table.

The rest of the band wasn't here yet. Music blasted over the sound system, the house lights were down. A smattering of people hung at the bar. Phil was settling into his groove. I sat at the back, alone at a table, glad for the distance between us.

Earlier today I had been reading about a celebrity rock n roll wife who split with her rock star husband of twenty years. She was battling alcohol and pill addictions in a hospital in California. The hospital representatives told us she was recovering well, in the ICU. I felt sad for her. She had loved and lost and surrendered herself to drown out her emptiness in pills and booze in a sea of loneliness, although maybe being married to a rock star was no less lonely in some weird way. I'd hate to share my husband with 3 million fans.

I checked out her photos from the past. She was blonde, petite, a real fashionista. She would wear cute, lacey outfits to awards shows, charity events and movie premiers. She was so pretty, a fragile doll now broken to pieces in a stark hospital bed, surrounded by stone faced doctors poking and prodding her back to life. Tragic. It was amazing what life could do you. Life could literally suck the life out of you.

Ian and Jon have arrived, moving in the bass amp gear and microphones. Jon was decked out in a black hoodie jacket over his white undershirt and Ian was decked out in a brown casual ensemble sporting flip-flops. Lady Gaga pounded on the speakers. I love Lady Gaga, what style, what panache, and what music. What a package, singer, performer, she is hot. It would be cool to be her, maybe for one day. It would be great to see the inside of her closet….

I wonder if she does normal things like buying food and doing laundry. I doubt those items on the to do list are high on her list of priorities.

Today at the check out line at Publix I saw a rag of Cher, she's having Chaz issues. Cher is so cool. I 'd love to be her forever. I would not want to be Chaz though, too messy.

Beth waited in the lounge of the Colony Hotel for Jon. The lounge was an open, airy courtyard filled with palm trees. An old, wooden bar lined the wall and the bartender was a throwback to rat pack days gone by. It was 12:30 am and his gig had been over for an hour. Tonight she was dressed up in a black cocktail dress, black choker and strappy black heels, a la Pretty Woman. She wanted to look as seductive as possible for Jon.

She watched as fish in the large fish tank by the bar swam in endless circles through mazes of rocks and coral. She toyed with her vodka and cranberry juice. She needed to be buzzed a bit before she saw him tonight. Some creepo guy at the end of the bar was giving her the eye. She stared at the fish, intently.

This was her last night in town before heading back to New York. Work was going well. Her boss Melanie was cool. She sometimes wondered if her boss was a lesbian, she kept prodding at her personal life, asking her what she was doing and who she was seeing. She still loved Jon. She wanted to make tonight special. She had a room upstairs at the hotel. The hotel was an old, magnificent 1920's building, with grand ballroom and nooks and crannies, libraries, billiard room, and swimming pool.

Her room had a king size bed in it, with crisp white linens and fluffy white towels in the bathroom. She had a candle by the bed and a bottle of red wine for later. She looked at her watch. Where was he?

The sound check was well underway. Jon was in a daze, coddling his guitar, swigging his beer, bathed in a red spotlight. Tracy Chapman played on the stereo, something about driving a fast car. The bartender, a pug nosed, bitchy blonde went ballistic on a customer and the sound man brought the levels up to speed in the monitors.

Jon was into a cool, funky groove on the guitar. He felt good tonight. Life sucked, no doubt. He had no car, a girlfriend on the edge of sanity, parents that still tried to control him and seemingly endless bad luck. He had no job and was living off his credit cars until they ran out. Then what? He was up against the odds. He really needed a break.

He couldn't handle another relapse by Beth. If she fucked up one more time he would close the door forever. Jon dreamed of making it big. His songs were good. The right ear balls hadn't heard his songs yet. No one recognized his talent. No one cared about him now that he was just a skinny, homeless, and no name punk kid. One day he'd be big. A Grammy award winning recording artist. The young chicks would flock to his shows. They would throw their Victoria Secrets G-strings at his feet and leave keys to their rooms. He'd wear designer rags and play on Letterman. One day. One day. One day.

One day he and Beth would settle down and have a couple of kids. He'd teach them guitar in between his gigs. He'd be bi-coastal, have an agent in Los Angeles and one in New York. He'd have a press agent handle his entire PR, he'd have an entourage. The once in awhile he would do the odd film. He'd transition from music to film like Johnny Depp did…..He kept telling himself all this as he scrounged for money for drinks and bummed cigarettes from his slowly dwindling group of friends.

Chapter 12

Stephanie parked the car and walked towards the large K Mart sign. K Mart, where smart shoppers shopped. She needed some new clothes. Cheap stuff to wear. Ian was playing tonight so she had the whole night to browse at her leisure without being nagged to hurry up and leave the store. Men were terrible browsers.

Her weight loss plan was beginning to pay off. Her face had slimmed down and she was down 1 size already. She was now a 14 but planned to get down to an 8. It would happen, it was all part of her master plan. She had found this awesome new protein diet on the Internet. She was cutting out all the breads, rice and other starched from her diet and eating only chicken, greens, nuts and fruits. It was working!!!

She was having doubts about Ian even though he did bring her flowers the other day. He still wasn't attentive enough. Sometimes she thought about leaving him but the thought of being alone scared her. The thought of being single scared her. She needed Ian. She would become the woman he wanted her to be. She would become superwoman.

Stephanie hit the racks and searched through some T-Shirts and tops. She picked out a pink T and a star-studded black belt. She found a pair of jeans for $6.00. this was a hot outfit! Soon her transformation would be complete. Then she would see. She'd have Ian begging for sex, she would make him worship her. She checked out with her new credit card. Ah, the joys of fresh credit. Only $27.00…..

Soon, soon, soon……

Phil was at my side on the break lamenting about Jon.

"He thinks he's a star."

"Maybe he will be."

"Then where are the people? The fans? He hasn't got any."

"I don't know."

"You don't tell the world you're going to be a star, the world tells you…."

"I know…He's young…"

Phil was hard on Jon. It was the voice of experience vs. the voice of youth. The show kicked off and Jon was rocking in the spotlight. Two of Jon's' fans walked in. Ugh! It was the chick I liked to call the Cougar. She was looking to jump his bones for sure. Phil said she was more like his Mom but I could see the calculating spark in her eyes every time he sang once of his yet to be discovered songs. She basically eyed Jon as her own private rock and roll star, her latch to fame. She never said hello to anyone, maybe because her Dad was some investment banker and this was her foray into slumming with the "artist".

Beth continued to wait at the bar. It was now 1:00 am. Still neither hide nor hair of Jon. The creepo at the other end of the bar came over.

“Hi…I’m James….I couldn’t help noticing how stunning you are. Nice dress.”

“Thanks…..” (Thanks you freak)

“Can I buy you a drink?”

“Ok, I’ll take a vodka and cranberry”(If you’re buying then why not)

“Anything you want, babe, anything.”

“Thanks.” (Loser)

James ordered the drink. He kept looking hungrily at her, licking his lips like he was going to eat her. He handed her the drink slowly, taking time to caress her hand.

“I can tell that you are waiting for someone”….

“Really? How can you tell?” (What the fuck?)

“The dress, the look in your eyes.. I hope that he doesn’t show so I can take you home.”

“Well. ….He’s coming so I guess you are out of luck tonight.” (Loser)

“A man can only hope.”

Beth was amused at the flirtation. Jon would walk in any minute now and catch her in the act. The she would be saved from this noodle head.

“Where are you from?” he asked her

“New York.”

“Oh, a big time city girl. Watch Sex and the City? I’d like to take a bite out of your apple.” He was so close to her she could feel him spitting on her.

She looked at him like he was out of his mind.

“Care for a dance?” he pressed on.

“Nope….Excuse me….”

Beth slunk away from the bar and into the ladies room. She washed her face with some cold water. She was feeling woozy from the drink. She dialed Jon’s’ cell number but it was off. She left a message.

“Babe…It’s me…I’ll be waiting in the room. It’s room 202. The Colony Hotel. See you soon. Bye”

Beth rode the elevator to her room. She opened the door. The room smelled like pineapple air freshener. She lit the candle by the bed and lay back. The sheets felt cool on her skin. Later Jon would be here. Later. Later. Later……

Jon held the guitar behind his head. He sang with anger and conviction. He wasn't kidding around tonight. Did anybody in this lea bitten bar give a damn about his music?

I sat and watched the show and wondered where Beth was. She was still in town. Jon dove into his next original tune, a Hendrix song. Phil and Ian were into it as well. The band was definitely grooving tonight. His voice was homey and familiar. He sang the lyrics effortlessly. He was on tonight. Where was Beth??? I often wondered about those two.

Sometimes I would see him with another girl, a girl he'd had a fling with. He always let everybody know that they had done it. That was one thing about being a band wife, you saw and heard it all. You knew all the backbiting, who drank too much, who stole the tip money, who had tacos for dinner, who was fucking up and who was in a pissy mood that night.

Jon had his fair share of conquest although generally he was pretty insecure around women. He seemed to have a fear of saying all the wrong things. I know he toyed with the idea of finding himself a "sugar mama", some rich chick that would set him up in a condo, buy him sports cars and guitars at Guitar Center. But then, didn't all broke musicians think like that?

But deep down in his heart he was a romantic. A true blue, one-woman man. The kind of man that would like to ride off in a convertible Mustang with his bride at his side. I saw him and Beth that way, but somehow circumstances beyond their control would fuck up their relationship.

Beth lay in bed dreaming. She was in a mansion, seated at a long dining table. A zebra with a reverends coat on sat beside her. Music played while they feasted on pheasant and figs. The zebra began playing a violin…..She was floating above the table…..She tossed and turned.

Jon played more Hendrix. The guitar was at a fever pitch. The sound was Godlike….I stared at Ian's' flip-flops onstage. The people at the bar ignored Jon. I watched Phil playing the drums….He would stare ahead and then sneak peeks at me. The room shook from the steady pounding of the drums. They were deafening.

A surfing video plays on the giant TV screen. Scenes of suntanned Gods splashing in the waves and girls in bikinis walking down the beach. Ride that wave dude. Freeze frame. I sip my Coke and spaced out. I've heard all these songs one hundred times before, I know every word, every note the band will play.

The band does their last song of the night. Just then the door opens and the most fucked up looking woman I have ever seen walks in. She's about six feet tall, has tits out to Toledo, she's dancing and waving her arms and falling on the stage. She throws herself at Jon's' feet and writhes around the floor on the stage. Guys at the bar grab her and pull her off the stage but she fights them off. She is strong, probably on smack or acid, she's tripping for sure.
She gets thrown out the door and the guys barricade the door. She's yelling and screaming and eating grass outside the club. She starts to strip, taking off her jeans a to reveal her pussy. She lies in the street and bends over, causing oncoming cars to stop and stare. The owner of the bar calls the cops. The cops come to take her away.

Now that the drama is over, the band can get back to packing up and getting the hell out. Phil waits nervously at the bar for the cash. This club pays cash. Cash is always a bonus. Checks suck because then you have to run it through the bank and maybe even declare it. Cash is king in music.

Jon packed up his guitar and amp. He had a few beers tonight, maybe a few too many. He was definitely buzzed. The guys had their chitchat about what a fucked up night it had been. Phil packed up his drums and stashed them away in the car. We were ready to leave. Another gig over.

Jon turned the key in his ignition. Lady Gaga played on the radio. He turned that shit right off. He checked his messages. Beth was waiting for him at her hotel. Shit! It was late…She would be pissed off. A cop from across the parking lot watched him. Jon pulled out onto the road and the cop stealthily followed. Jon didn't notice the white squad car behind him. He lit a cigarette and ran a stop sign in front of the 7-11. The cop put on his lights……He was busted.
Fuck. Fuck. Fuck……

Chapter 13

We were playing again tonight, two nights in a row. Jon was out of jail. Looking bleary eyed and worn down. We were all running on a few hours of sleep after the bang up night last night. Everyone was still buzzing about it. Tonight was a gig at South Shores, a local hang out on Lake Worthless, Florida. I was sitting in a booth, watching football as the guys set up. I am not much of a football fan, I jut like to imagine the players in the locker room after the game. Tom Brady? Sure…….

I've never dated a football player, I am not that kind of sports trophy wife. Sometimes I watch basketball Wives on TV. It's a dog eat dog world of nasty basketball wives vying each other for fame, fortune and trophy husbands, many of who are unfaithful to their opportunistic wives.

My husband is far from most would call a trophy husband. He is a reader, a tinkerer, a technician and an artist…He's a genius of sorts. I like to consider him that. He also can nag and get on my nerves. If we were major celebrities we probably would have been divorced long ago. No woman would put up with the amount of hassling that he hassles me. It's all a compromise really. I know I get on his nerves too. We are both imperfect.

The band is setting up. Reggae music plays in the background. I am thirsty as hell and need refreshment. Phils' hooch is in my bag, his alcohol fix for tonight. He also brought a weed cookie tonight, hope he doesn't freak out if he eats it and ends up like that woman last night, stripping out in the road, baring his bony ass to oncoming traffic.

I try to imagine the lives of famous band wives like Yoko Ono, Heather Locklear, Pamela Anderson, Heidi Klum, Christie Brinkley, Valerie Bertinelli. I'll bet these women have stories to blow you away about their famous musician husbands. They are the bad boys of rock and roll.

Tonight I'm wearing a beautiful heart shaped pendant Phil gave me for Christmas. He picked it out for me and surprised me with it. I love surprises. Sometimes I think I like to give surprises more than receive them. I guess that's part of the control freak in me that does that.

Al the local flower man is here giving out flowers. He tells us that he's been married for fifty years up until his wife died. He gives us a rose for our anniversary, even though it isn't our anniversary. Sweet man. I love my rose.

Some say love, it is a river
That drowns the tender reed.
Some say love, it is a razor
That leaves your soul to bleed.
Some say love, it is a hunger,
An endless aching need.
I say love, it is a flower,
And you its only seed.

Phil is all revved up tonight, the testosterone pumping in his veins. He has this phobia about people touching me. When you are the wife of a band member, people touch you, grab you, kiss you, shake your hand, kiss your hand, hug you…..It's hard to escape them. Phil has some very intense issues……It's hard to believe we've been married for fourteen years.

I study the drink menu and ponder what to order. There's the Tiki Colada, with Bacardi Cherry Rum or the New Orleans Hurricane with orange juice, passion fruit, lime juice and Grenadine…that sounds good. Might as well get buzzed and listen to the band.

Phil comes over to get his double shot of Captain Morgan and sprite. He needs the injection of alcohol to calm him down so he can zone out into playing. The place is buzzing with people, laughter and music. I wonder how the night will go.

Beth arrived at LFK and hailed a cab to Brooklyn. It was a cold January night and she felt alone. Jon had dumper her again. This was it for her. She didn't buy his DUI story at all, it was lame. She paid the cabbie and walked up the steps to the brownstone. She opened her door and went in, shaking the slush of her shoes. Home at last. She checked her messages.

"Hi dear, this is Mom…call me when you get in. I was worried about you."

Beep

"Beth, its me, Jon….Call me."

Beep

"Beth, this is Melanie. I need you in the office Monday morning at 8:30 for a meeting."

Beep.

Beth sat on the couch and curled up in a warm, blue blanket. What she needed now was a nice hot shower and a warm cup of herbal tea. She felt as though she was coming down off of a high. Life would go on. Screw Jon, he was such a conceited, self-absorbed jerk.

Stephanie sat at the bar watching the guys. Her friends Star and Lauren were there, both were in the process of breaking up with their boyfriends who were also in other bands.

"He told me he needs more space." moaned Star.

"You're the best thing that ever happened to him. What is he? Nuts?" Stephanie said, eyeing the perfect blonde in short mini dress beside her.

"Men are such pricks," lamented Lauren "I don't even know why I like penises…."

Stephanie agreed, though she still was in love with Ian.

I went over and gave Stephanie a big hug. Tonight would be a major girls night out, a man bashing, drinking party. The band started. People were dancing. I wondered if there would be any nudity tonight.

Lauren was bumping and grinding on the dance floor, making goo-goo eyes at Jon. She had a boyfriend, a bass player named Ed. Ed was an old guy. Lauren thought Jon was young and cute. Plus, she was wasted.

I cornered Stephanie by the ladies room.

"How are you girl?"

"Good…"

"How's it going with Ian?"

“It’s alright but I really need to kick some ass.”

“I hear you……

“I’m planning on making some major changes…”

“Alright, can’t wait to hear all about it.”

I smiled. Stephanie was the best. We walked back to the lounge. Jon began singing an original song and dedicated it to Beth in a weird, sarcastic way. It felt like the end. I had heard about the fuck up last night. Too bad those two were always the victims of some weird fateful co-incidence. I guess that time would tell, if there was any left.

Some chicks from a nearby table requested that the guys in the band take off their shirts.

“Three for the price of one.” They yelled out.

It was going to be one of those nights. Jon stripped off his shirt and a woman put a $20.00 in his jeans.

There was nudity after all. Where was my cell phone camera?

Chapter 14

Another Friday night, another gig. Last night was a humdinger. I spent the night talking with Stephanie. Jon showed up at the gig but forgot his guitar, so Ian drove him back to his place one half hour away. The night was off to a rocky start for the band.

Stephanie was in good spirits, talkative and trying to control her asthma with an inhaler. She was telling me about her psycho Mom, how she wanted to make up with her and tell her that she loved her unconditionally, but was afraid. I don't blame her for being afraid. When somebody has hurt you all your life you tend to stay away. It's like getting your hand burned on the stove, after awhile you either fear the pain or become numb to it.

We talked about Phil and I. Stephanie thought we need more space between us, her space and his space kind of space. I tried to convince her that this is how Phil likes it, but she had her opinion of our relationship. It's funny to see how others see your relationship. They usually have a negative view of it, like he should treat you better or you should get out more by yourself, or something like that. Other sees misery where we see happiness. I guess it must have been my fault for complaining about things as we women do. I should try to complain less. Bitching. I am guilty.

The guys played great tonight. I caught the odd mistake here and there. It was cool. No nude dances this week, no drama. The place was pretty quiet for a Friday night.

After a set or two, Stephanie and I slipped outside to the tiki bar where sat by the fire and inhaled smoke. Stephanie let loose and confided in me that she and Ian were experimenting with hallucinogenic drugs. She described her experiences to me:

"It was like, so cool…"

"Cool…"

"It was like time slowed down, like one minute lasted for two weeks."

"Man…Sounds bizarre"

"It was so cool. I could feel my mind opening up."

"Wow, sounds so cool…..I think I'd be scared to try it."

"I did it to let go of some shit from the past."

"Did it work?"

"Yes."

"Yeah?"

"It like, erased some walls in my mind."

Then Ian came out and joined us. Ian was so mellow, he was holding Stephanie's' hand while she talked. You could feel the trust between then had gotten stronger. Ian was into experimenting. I was too afraid to try anything. And Phil was already enough of a basket case, he didn't need drugs.

We talked about soul retrieval and how that works It very interesting that you can get back parts of your life, chunks of your life that you thought were gone with the help of a shaman or maybe even with these drugs.

Sometimes when I talk to Stephanie I start to remember things from my past. I listen to her talk about her childhood and I think about mine. But she had such a tragic childhood and I had a happy childhood so it's hard to relate to the horror stories she tells me. I wish she could reconcile with her mother. She has all but given up.

We said goodnight, the guys got paid, and we hugged……

Beth sat at the conference table and sipped her Starbucks Café au Lait. Melanie was talking about a new program for kids. Beth thought about Jon. She was fantasizing about the last time they made love, about how he made her feel. She missed him. She still wanted him.

The door opened and in walked Chad. He was the newest person on their team and he had a big crush on Beth and she could feel it.

"Hi Chad."

"Beth….Always a pleasure."

Melanie glanced over at them annoyed. "I'm only going over this once so please pay attention." she chirped.

Chad and Beth smiled at each other. He slipped her a note under the table.

It read:
"Dinner tonight at Thai Palace?"

She folded the note in her palm. Well, he was gorgeous and rich and dug her….She smiled and nodded yes.

I was busy working on my third children's story. I had the stories written but no illustrations yet. I'd been trying to find a publisher but all I was getting was rejections across the board. I was convinced that if I could get my book to the right publisher I could be a successful author of the children's series, "Serengetti"

I looked up a New York publisher who was accepting submissions and emailed him the stories. It would take about six weeks to get a response. These publishers were so difficult. It was hard to get your foot in the door.

Phil was in the next room working on his golf swing. He was spending every walking minute practicing and reading books like “Slot Swing” and “Bad Golf”. If he wasn’t playing drums he was playing golf.

I was on the phone with my mother. She was getting older and facing difficult things in her life like dealing with retirement issues and not being able to walk up stairs and things like that. It was hard to deal with your parents getting older. Personally, I was on the 100-year plan. I planned to be 100. Then I can die in peace. Hope I make my mark.

Chad and Beth sat facing each other in the Thai Palace. It was a serene setting, with water fountains trickling water and bamboo blinds creating intimate seating arrangements. The table had a crisp, clean tablecloth on it and the waitress brought them a small salad.

“I love the food here, Chef Allen makes a dynamite curry sauce.”

“Sounds yummy”

“So, tell me more about you.”

“Well, like what?”

“Are you involved with anyone?”

“No, I was…..I’m just getting out of a relationship.”

“Poor guy….Must have been hard to lose a girl like you”

“I don’t think he feels that way…I guess I was just too irresponsible for him.”

“Hmmmmnnnn…I’m just coming out of a relationship myself.”

“Oh really?”

“Yes, I was with my ex for seven years. She wanted the four kids, the house in Connecticut and the whole deal.”

“And you didn’t?”

“I’m an immature jerk I guess. No. No way.”

“Don’t be so hard on yourself….’

He looked around the restaurant.

“Can I kiss you?” He leaned over and kissed her on the lips.

“Thanks, that was nice…”

“What would Melanie think?”

“Melanie? She’s a lesbian.”

“I thought so!!!”

“She’s had her eye on you babe.”

“Glad you got to me first!”

They laughed.

“So why did you break off your relationship with your boy friend?”

“I just….I just, ah..Fucked up. It’s kind of personal.”

“Ok, sorry to be so nosy.”

“Alright….I guess we should go now. Have to be at work tomorrow.”

Beth and Chad walked down the street. It was dark. The odd ambulance went by. He hailed her a cab.

“See you tomorrow gorgeous.” He planted another kiss on her lips.

“See you.”

Beth sat back in the cab. Her first date since Jon had dumper her went well. He was a bit pushy, she thought. She'd have to hold him back. She wasn't ready for more heartache yet.

Chapter 15

We were broke tonight and it was dinnertime. I suggested tacos. Phil suggested burritos. So I set out to the grocery store to make some hot and delicious burritos. I only had ten dollars, so it was a bit of a challenge.

I bought the meat and the tortilla and some corn and tomatoes. Everything looked good as the cashier tallied up the purchases. It was raining out side so I ran to the car with the groceries and made my way home.

At home I chopped up the tomatoes and lettuce and simmered the meat in a big pan. I set out little plates on the table, a la Sante Fe Style cuisine. I thought that the plates looked colorful and festive. I lit a candle for some romance.

So Mr Big Cheese comes to eat. He's like "What is this?" I am like, "Dinner. It's the burritos." First thing he does is burn himself on the candle. Now incensed he tries to make a burrito. He opens his mouth to eat it and it spills all over him. Now my notion of this being a romantic, festive meal is over. He's all upset, swearing and carrying on.

So much for the burrito dinner. There are some leftovers though…….I will eat them later.

Last night we were out at a club where Phil had a drumming gig. I happened to be sitting next to an interesting woman whose husband was also a drummer. They were from California. She was a band wife too…..

Her name was Ingrid and she was telling me all about California. They had lived there for twenty years and they loved it there. She had been living in San Diego for awhile. She knew La Jolla and The Del Coronado Hotel. Her family had been in the hotel building business and she was telling me about her exotic lifestyle growing up, traveling to locales all over the world and meeting rich and famous musicians.

She met Janis Joplin once, when she was fourteen in San Juan, Puerto Rico at the El San Joan Hotel. Janis was my idol. I have been there and always loved that hotel. It was a magnificent place.

So she was telling me about San Francisco and wine country and how her husband would play a gig in a vineyard and so on. Sounded so nice. I just wanted to move right there and then to someplace new, someplace exciting. It would be nice to see mountains, drive along the Pacific Coast Highway and put some flowers in your hair.

If you're going to San Francisco
Be sure to wear some flowers in your hair

If you're going to San Francisco
You're gonna meet some gentle people there

For those who come to San Francisco
Summertime will be a love-in there
In the streets of San Francisco
Gentle people with flowers in their hair

All across the nation such a strange vibration
People in motion
There's a whole generation with a new explanation
People in motion people in motion

For those who come to San Francisco
Be sure to wear some flowers in your hair
If you come to San Francisco
Summertime will be a love-in there

If you come to San Francisco
Summertime will be a love-in there

Then she was talking about Hollywood and all the movie stars and show business in general. Her husband had played many high profile gigs there. Man, I wish I could go there someday soon. I know I would love it……..Life always seemed more exciting somewhere else. I wonder if Phil would want to go and start a new life somewhere else?

Chapter 16

Another night, another gig. Tonight Phil was hassling me about my snoring. I know I snore, I can't help it. He claims hehasn't had a decent nights sleep in ten years. So me being me, I turn around and hassle him about his slurping his drink. Tit for tat. Of course, this incenses him and he starts ranting and raving like a lunatic. This is what I call the pre-gig behavior. Usually it is the actual unloading of equipment that sets off the real temper tantrums but this is the pre-stuff, the nastiness before the gig.

Being a band wife is not all its cracked up to be. Besides being a wife you also have to be a nurse, a mommy, a roadie, a cook, a therapist and a sex starved groupie. Men in bands want you to worship them, tell them they look great, tell them they are great, tell them they sounded great, etc etc etc. It never ends. The huge egos.

Stephanie is here tonight at South Shores. She is busy sucking down a strawberry rum runner when I find her at the band table. She says she's had a hard day. At least she didn't have to deal with a ranting lunatic on the way to the gig.

Phil joins us and goes on a new rant about what a failed species humans are. Talk about Mr. Pessism. Stephanie raises her eyebrows at me in a "wow" gesture. That's ok, we all know he is out of his mind. My mind keeps wandering back to last nights conversation about California, about the beautiful people there, the land and the mountains. Ingrid also told me about the women there, how gorgeous they are, tall, exotic breeds from Russia and Yugoslavia and Romani with gold bangles on their wrists and tight, sexy skirts with high heeled stillettos. She told me that these women capitalize on their looks. I'll bet…They are all looking for Mr Goodbar, their rich American husband to foot the bills.

Who am I kidding? I feel too old to go to California. My "star" days are over now. If I was out there I would cast for the old mother role in the movies. "Yes, I am here for the part of the older woman" I would tell the casting agent.

It's five minutes to show time. The guys are squawking about some rock drummer. Jon lights up a cigarette and looks nervously around the crowd. The place is full of people. It's windy and hopefully it won't rain, since it's an outdoor gig.

Stephanie checked her cell phone. It was a call from her friend Mike. He owned a really cool tattoo shop. She was planning on getting a tattoo for her birthday, a really beautiful Celtic design she made. Ian liked it, that was all that mattered. She thought back to the first time she had heard Ian's voice on the phone. It was love at first listen. She had felt instantly connected to him, even before she met him…..Love was strange.

I sat and watched Jon onstage, prancing around and holding his guitar above his head. Some people dropped money in the makeshift tip jar. I thought of what he might become, maybe a teenage idol for young girls, like a page out of Teen magazine. Send Jon your thoughts and dreams…….He had potential. He was no Justin Bieber, he was more like a Beatle….. He was cute and adorable, except for his excessive drinking and total sarcastic wit. If only he had a manager to clean up his bad boy image and make him marketable.

I wondered what being the wife of a really famous rock star husband would be like. Would it be all limousines, jets, first class hotels and having to endure love starved fans? I could handle it. After being with a no-name stardom sure played out nice and sweet. Of course there would be pitfalls, disappointments, betrayals and jealousy. But these elements were already in play for no money, might as well go for the big bucks.

The band was on break, talking about Jimmy Hendrix.

'Thank God Hendrix had recordings because God, he was probably so out of tune half the time."

"He was blasted for sure."

"He probably recorded that shit tripping dude." Ian said

This could go on for hours….Phil changed the subject.

"I think I'm going to get into Zen." What a surprise!

“Try Chi” suggested Stephanie

“Maybe drugs.” said Phil

The guys were always talking about how they fucked up. Perfectionists, all of them. Yet they were all so imperfect.

“I need more hooch.” said Phil

I poured him some hooch. The band started playing again. It was a heavy rock number. Skank alert!!! Skank alert!!!

A wild, hippie looking chick meets Donna Summers starts dancing in front of the band, wearing a grey fringed poncho top, skin tight jeans and gold lame shoes. Then some disco boy Johnny Saturday Night fever guy joins her and the two are strutting their stuff in front of the band. I can see them smiling. This is good entertainment! Jon plays a solo and Phil pounds on the drums. Ian keeps it all in check with steady base. The chick is spinning around and clapping her hands. Denny Terrio would be proud. Dance Fever!

Jon plays well tonight, despite his cold. He’s been blowing away, says he caught the cold from a chick. No doubt, since he’s been on the prowl for some tail since Beth left him.

The band rocks to “I Wanna Be Sedated”. It is a perfect night, just cool enough to wear a hoodie. I look up and now yet another skanker is dancing, this time a blonde about seventy-five pounds heavier than the last one. Soon a drunken man on a unicycle joins her. It is a freak show…. I can't wait to get home…

I finished up my kid's story and mailed it out to yet another publisher, this time in New York. With every self-addressed, self-stamped envelope my hopes and dreams seemed to diminish as the weeks went by with no responses or rejection letters from publishers.

Stephanie couldn't believe her luck. Chloe Case was having a contest, looking for the next young, hot designer. She feverishly sketched up her bag design and colored the sketches with her permanent markers. She loved her bag design. It was well crafted, yet natural, and functional yet aesthetically pleasing. It was a bad ahead of its time. With compartments for all necessities, it was every woman's dream bag. She hoped that Chloe would notice her. She scanned and emailed the designs to New York, the big apple, the city of dreams.

Beth walked along the river by herself. It was sunset, her favorite time of day. It seemed that the city slowed down a bit, to bask in the glory in the colors of the sky. She had a lot to think about, Jon, Chad, her new job and her own demons. She felt alone. She felt like drinking again, drinking just to make it all go away so she wouldn't have to deal with it anymore.

Beth knew she had to stop herself. She walked to a building and opened the door. She walked down the long, white hallway into a room. Some people were sitting at a long gray table. There was heavy smoke in the room. She sat alone in the corner and shrank down into her seat. A man stood at the front of the table. He looked at her.

"What is your name?"

She stood up.

"My name is Beth and I am an alcoholic" and sat down.
It felt good to say it. It felt good to come clean and let it all out. The people in the room clapped. Someone patted her on the back.

"It's alright Child," a soft voice said. It was a tall, black woman.

"My name is Grace." She held her hand in hers.

Beth smiled. It was going to be all right.

Weeks went by and there was no word from any publishers. I was pretty much over it. I came home from work one night and Phil was playing his guitar. He was in a mellow mood.

“Hi.” he said

“Hey! How was your day?”

“Good, the mail came today. This ones for you.”

He held out an ecru colored envelope. It was postmarked New York. I opened it up. It read:

We would like to congratulate you on your submission “Serengeti” to Rainbow Publishing. We are proud to include your work into our catalog of children’s fiction. Our publisher Ivan Ivansky would like a meeting in our New York office on Monday May 14. Please respond to us at (212) 555-1010 for details.

Oh my God! Acceptance at last! I started to cry. Phil looked over at me.

“Babe, what is it?”

“My book….”

“Ah, forget that book…”

“No! They accepted my book! The publisher wants to meet me in New York.”

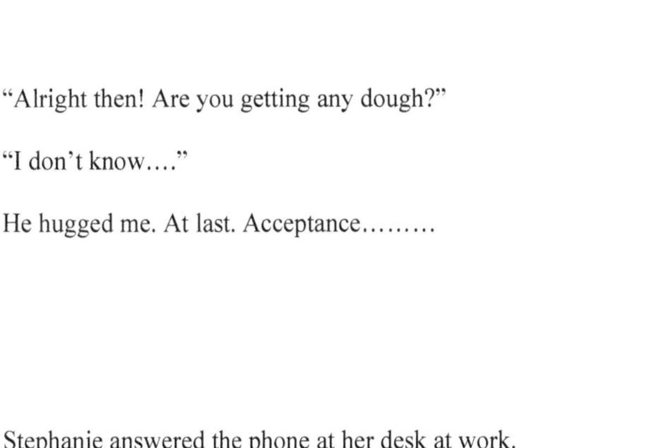

"Alright then! Are you getting any dough?"

"I don't know…."

He hugged me. At last. Acceptance………

Stephanie answered the phone at her desk at work.

"Collins & Collins."

"May I speak to Stephanie Burk?" a mans voice said on the phone.

"This is she. Who is calling?" she asked guardedly.

"This is Marc le Blanc from Chloe Cases' office in New York"

"Yes? This is Stephanie."

"Congratulations, your handbag design has been chosen as the handbag design for the future."

Stephanie thought maybe this was Ian playing a prank on her.

“Ian, cut it out, you litle shit!”

“Pardon me?” the voice on the other end was quiet.

“This is Chloe Cases’ assistant, Marc. I am totally serious Ms Burk.”

“Oh my God!. I am so sorry. I just can’t believe it....”

“We are calling you to tell you that we will be mailing you a ticket to come to our designers showcase Monday May 14. I will follow up with all the details. Congratulations!”

Stephanie sank into her seat. She was in shock. Her bag won? New York? Chloe Case? It was way too good to be true. Her boss stuck his head out of the office.

“Who was that on the phone?” he asked.

“It was for me, a personal call…”

“Everything alright?”

“Yes…It certainly is…I might need a few days off…”

Stephanie couldn’t believe it. She won. She felt incredible happiness. Suddenly all her pain slipped away. Her mother, Ian, her weight, her past, the drama, and the years she felt useless. Now she was a winner. Someone had spotted her talent.

Beth arrived at the door to her brownstone. She felt a great sense of satisfaction that she had gone to her first meeting on her own. This was her first step towards recovery. A small orange kitten was there in the corner. She went over to it and tried to pet it. It let her touch it.

"Hey little guy…what are you doing here alone?"

"Meow."

"Are you hungry?"

"Meow."

She scooped him up and took him inside the apartment. She set him down on the floor and watched as he sniffed around the furniture.

Her messages were blinking.

Beep

"Beth? Hi, it's Heather…. You are not going to believe this but I got a publishing deal for my book and I am coming to New York….Call me!"

Beep

“Beth, its your mother dear. I have been trying to reach you….Give me a call. I have something to tell you.”

Beep

“Beth, Steph here. I am coming to New York…….I have so much to tell you….Bye.”

Beth sat on the sofa and played with the cat. Sounded like a lot of excitement was coming her way.

Stephanie and I were scheduled to fly to New York Friday night for the long weekend. Phil drove us to the airport, ranting and raving about publishers and designers and how he mistrusted large corporations. We took it all in with a grain of salt. Nothing would ruin our mood now.

“Don’t do anything I wouldn’t do.” he warned.

“No…Baby…….”

“Remember, these people are just using you for your talent. If they were so great they would have come up with these ideas themselves.” He kept on his tirade.

We smiled at each other. It was going to be a band wives reunion. We were so excited. We arrived at the airport terminal. I gave Phil a long kiss goodbye.

“Call me.”

"I will."

We hugged one last time and Stephanie and I walked into the terminal to check our bags. Then we sat around at Starbucks and paid for an overinflated cup of strong coffee before our flight.

"Do you believe this?" I asked.

"I know. I cannot believe this."

"I can't wait to see Beth."

"It'll be like old times, just the three of us."

We boarded our flight after an extensive security screening and I settled into my seat. I looked out the window. Goodbye sunshine, hello New York! The flight took off and once we were in the air I watched an in flight movie without the sound because I didn't want to spend the six bucks to rent the headphones. What happened to free perks? Even a lousy sandwich cost $11.00 now.

I fell asleep and when I woke up people were on their feet as the plane pulled into the gate at La Guardia. We hailed a cab to Brooklyn. There was energy here in New York. We felt it as our excitement mounted in intensity.

Beth was standing outside the brownstone as the cab pulled up. She was holding a little kitten in her arms. She had a big smile on her face.

“Look what the cat dragged in!” she said.

We all hugged and kissed.

“Come on inside.”

We followed her down the hall to her apartment. I was surprised at how cool it was inside. It was decorated sparsely but tastefully.

“You guys! I can’t believe you are here!” Beth smiled.

“We can’t either.” I said

“How are the guys?”

“Same old shit.”

Next came the loaded question. “How’s Jon doing?”
I spared her the details of Jon’s philandering and his DUI.

“He’s good, been playing better and better all the time. He’s like a real rock star now.”

“Oh yeah?” she said curiously.

“Yeah, but you can do better.”

“I don’t know. I miss him. I think about him a lot.”

"Yeah…I am sure he thinks about you too,"

"Come on, let's get to bed. We have a lot to do."

We spent the weekend shopping and wandering through Central Park. We hung out at Beths' apartment in Brooklyn and had a bitching session while we put on our mineral clay mud masks. My mask was hardening, causing deep straits on my face as I laughed, trying hard to keep a straight face. We were slightly buzzed on a bottle of white Zinfandel. We decided to do our toes.

"I want the Sugar Daddy" said Stephanie

"I'm doing mine in Green Apple" said Beth

"Give me the ravishing red." I said.

I drank some more Zinfandel. It tickled my nose. I noticed that Beth popped a pill during the night, but I didn't want to say anything, I wasn't her mother.

"You know what Ian did last week?" said Stephanie

"He made you dinner." I guessed.

"Better than that, he bought me flowers."

"Really? For no reason?"

"Yup."

“Are you sure he’s not having an affair?” said Beth

“That’s a pessimistic thought.” I said. “You know what Phil did?”

“I can’t imagine.” Said Stephanie

“We go into a big fight and then afterwards he apologized.”

“Wow.”

“It’s hard to imagine….What were you arguing about?” asked Beth

“He blames me for his troubles. Like I am the root of all the problems in his life.”

“That’s heavy dudette.”

“Yeah, I am glad he apologized though. It made me feel better.”

We both looked at Beth, waiting for her to own up to a confession about Jon. She pet the cat behind its ears.

“Jon is in the dog house. I don’t know if he’ll ever come out after leaving me at the hotel that night.”

We sighed. Young love……Our toenails were dry and our mud masks were cracking. It was time to rinse off. Girl time was important. I wondered how the guys were doing…..

Jon was checking the PA system. "Test, test, one , two…..Test." It sounded good….Ian was farting around with his bass rig and Phil was watching Super Bowl reruns. Tonight was their first night at this gig. It was a good gig, one hundred bucks per man. Nice pocket change.

Phil dialed his phone. I picked up.

"What are you mugs up to?"

"Getting beautiful."

"Don't get too good looking now, I might have to come and shoot somebody."

"We're going to make popcorn and watch 27 Dresses."

"Okay, love you…I've got to play."

I went into the kitchen and checked the cabinets for popcorn. There was some Orville Reddenbocher kernels in the back of the cabinet. I filled a pot with oil and let it heat up on the stove. All of a sudden I heard shrieking coming from the bathroom I ran inside.

"What is it?"

“Theres a frigging frog in the toilet.” Screamed Beth

“What?” I took a look in side the toilet bowl. There was a big giant frog in the toilet bowl.

“Oh shit!” Quick!!! Get something?”

The apartment was staring to fill with smoke.

“What’s burning?” Beth cried.

“Oh shit!! The popcorn!!!!!”

I ran into the kitchen and doused the pan with water. Then I took a pair of salad tongs and carried them into the bathroom, snapping them impatiently.

“Okay you sucker. You gots to go frogman….” I picked the frog up with the tongs and carried him to the balcony.

“You’re just lucky nobody took a shit on you Toadster.”

Monday morning came and we all took the train into the city. We all had separate appointments to catch. I headed for Seventh Avenue. Stephanie was headed uptown to Madison Avenue and Beth was headed to Midtown to her job.

Stephanie's heart pounded as she opened the door to Chloe Cases' world. She felt like an intruder crashing a private party, a woman in rags where others were supermodels dressed in evening gowns. She entered the showroom. It was a pristine palace of fashion.

"Hello. Welcome to Chloe Case."

"Hi. I am Stephanie Burk.... I won a contest....I have a nine o'clock appt."

"Welcome. Chloe is expecting you. Follow me please."

Stephanie followed the assistant up to an open loft workspace. There were mannequins clad in partially finished designs, bolts of fabric and sewing stuff all over the floor. Chloe was a tall, bony woman dressed in red leather jeans and and a white cotton blouse with red cowboy boots. Her long blonde hair was held back in a single ponytail, almost touching her waist. She turned to greet her with a big smile.

"Hi Stephanie, congratulations.... I love, love, love your design for the handbag collection.

"It's been in my head for a long time."

"Let me tell you about the new fall collection I want to feature the handbag in...

I found 700 Seventh Avenue and looked up the name of the publisher on the index. My heart was pounding as I rode the marble clad elevator to the 14th floor. I couldn't believe this moment was really coming true. The doors opened and I was bombarded by another world. The world of kids publishing. Book covers lined the walls of the publishing house. I walked over to the receptionist.

"I am Heather Guest, here to see Mr. Ivansky." I said nervously.

"Please have a seat and he will be out in a moment."

I sat on the leather sofa and looked at all of the famous authors. I could feel my palms getting sweaty. A tall, thin man appeared in the doorway. He was wearing jeans and a sweater and holding a coffee mug in one hand.

"Heather? Good to meet you. I am Ivan." He shook my hand heartily.

"Come into my office."

I followed him down the hallway into a large corner office overlooking Manhattan. He had pictures of his wife and kids on his credenza and the walls of the office were filled with books of all shapes and sizes.

"Care for some coffee?" he asked

“No thanks.” I was afraid I might spill it on myself.

“I must say that I really enjoyed your book. It was interesting and playful and very imaginative.”

“Thank you.”

“We would like to give you this. For starters.”
He handed me an envelope. I opened it and took out a check for $5000.00

“An advance.” he said.

“I don’t know what to say. I’ve never been paid for my writing before.” I couldn’t believe it. What would Phil say?

“Well, keep on writing and you’ll get more. I guarantee.”

I sighed. Life was good. Life was really good.

That night we three women went out to celebrate at the Rainbow Room atop Rockefeller. We were dressed to the nines in our short mini-dresses and pumps. The lounge was elegant and subdued and had a wonderful view of Manhattan. We ordered some cocktails, except for Beth who had cranberry juice.

“To us!”

We toasted.

I sat back and felt content. What more could I ask for? I was in love with my best friend; I had a book deal and was on top of the world with three of my closest friends. The band played a song. Someone tapped me on the shoulder. It was Phil standing there dressed up in a dark suit.

"Care for a dance?"

I was shocked. Behind him were Ian and Jon, decked out in fancy clothes. Ian took Stephanie's hand and he led her to the dance floor. Jon hugged Beth and they followed us. The band played "Stairway to Heaven" and we all swayed to the music.

This is what it meant to be a band wife and to come into our own. Sometimes dreams really do come true.

www.ingramcontent.com/pod-product-compliance
Ingram Content Group UK Ltd.
Pitfield, Milton Keynes, MK11 3LW, UK
UKHW020220250726
13967UKWH00001B/110

9 781300 420958